Who Lives in...
ALLIGATOR SWAMP?

Who Lives in... ALLIGATOR SWAMP?

Ron Hirschi

Photographs by
Galen Burrell

A *WHERE ANIMALS LIVE* BOOK

Dodd, Mead & Company • New York

Published by Dodd, Mead & Company, Inc.,
71 Fifth Avenue, New York, N.Y. 10003
Printed in Hong Kong by South China Printing Company
Designed by Charlotte Staub

1 2 3 4 5 6 7 8 9 10

Library of Congress Cataloging-in-Publication Data

Hirschi, Ron.
Who lives in—alligator swamp?

(A Where animals live book)
Summary: Text and photographs portray early morning in a swamp as the animals begin their day's activities.
1. Swamp fauna—Juvenile literature. 2. Swamp fauna—United States—Juvenile literature. [1. Swamp animals]
I. Burrell, Galen, ill. II. Title. III. Series.
QL114.5.H57 1987 597.6 87-9012
ISBN 0-396-09123-7
ISBN 0-396-09124-5 (pbk.)

For Tommy

Follow me
down the swamp rabbit's
path in the pale,
morning light.

Peek through the rabbit's brier patch
to where the sun shines brightly,
over the old blue heron's shoulder,
past the thrasher's lookout perch,

and beyond land's edge
where the alligator waits—
silently for now.

The old alligator floats
motionless as a log,

while a redstart and an oriole
fly up to greet the sun.

The towhee watches as

the morning's golden glow lights

every corner of the swamp.

Egrets dance and
the blackbird's wake-up call
stirs the other swamp
animals to life.

Who is rustling the reeds, rushes, and swamp potato plants beneath the bobcat's watchful eyes?

Is it the long-legged rail, poking for snails in the soft, thick mud?

Is it the bobolink, cracking seeds
as he clings to the
narrow stems?

The bright-faced gallinule?

Or the little green heron,
fishing for breakfast?

No! It is a baby alligator,
creeping through
the swamp.

The baby alligator
crawls onto a log, then
slips into the water.

Swimming out beyond

the anhinga's lily patch,

past the spoonbill's

protected cove.

He goes to
alligator island
where the old alligator
has crawled ashore.

Can you hear
his thundering
R-R-ROAR!?

AFTERWORD
for Parents and Teachers, Big Brothers and Sisters

Animals of the forest, marsh, lake, stream, grassland, and even the sea live together in swamps. Nowhere else can you see so much life!

In the American Southeast, alligator swamps are especially exciting places to visit and most of the animals appearing in this book were photographed in an accessible example, the Savannah National Wildlife Refuge in Georgia.

Alligators and crocodiles are the only surviving relatives of the reptile group (Archosauria) that included the dinosaurs. American alligators were once very near extinction due to the high demand for their skins. With protection from hunting and protection for their swamp homes in North and South Carolina, Georgia, Florida, Alabama, Mississippi, Arkansas, Louisiana, and Texas, they will continue to survive.

American crocodiles are far less abundant. In the United States crocodiles live mainly in the Everglades National Park region of Florida. They can be told from alligators by their more slender snouts and by the presence of two teeth in the lower jaws that are visible when their mouths are closed.

Many other animals live in swamps that occur along the Northeast Atlantic, the Pacific Coast, and in wet inland areas, especially along rivers and streams. These include the bald eagles that return each year to Pacific Northwest coastal swamps that form where rivers meet the sea.

We hope this introduction to the beauty of the swamp animals will encourage young people to care for the future of these special places.